Raising

My

Manchild

By

T. Grow

Foreword By L.C. Smith

Photography: Dokk Savage Photography |www.dokksavagephotography.com

Cover Design: Heidi Rudolph | www.heidirudolph.com

Edited By: Rikari E.

Printed in The United States of America

ISBN: 978-1-7372946-0-3 (PB)

ISBN: 978-1-7372946-1-0 (ePUB)

T DOT Grow

Table of content

Chapter 1: The Disclaimer 9

Chapter 2: Bitter Beginnings 11

Chapter 3: Finding Peace 16

Chapter 4: The Release 20

Chapter 5: Moving Forward 24

Chapter 6: Purposeful Healing 29

Chapter 7: An Unpopular Truth 33

Chapter 8: Planting Mustard Seeds 41

Chapter 9: Harvest 45

Chapter 10: This too Shall Pass 49

Chapter 11: A Change Is Gonna Come 54

Chapter 12: Giants Do Fall 62

Chapter 13: Be Encouraged 67

Dedication

To my son Jaden, you are my reason and the greatest hero I will ever believe in. Thank you for teaching me and trusting me. I am and will always be resoundingly proud; proud to parent you and ever more so proud of you. Keep rising to your own greatness.

Foreword

It is an honor to write this foreword, not only because La Toya Grow and her manchild have been adopted into our Real Fathers Making a Difference family, but also because of her fighting single mama spirit. That's right, her single mama fighting spirit! Like most single moms, having that tenacity to go hard for their children regardless of the circumstances. I'm not a single mom, hell I'm not even a woman, but unfortunately I know a lot of single mothers. I am director of an organization that works with young men without a strong father's presence and our phone constantly rings from mothers seeking support for their families.

This book captures all the reasons God placed this purpose within my soul. I've seen the struggle of a single mother, and I've lived the life of a fatherless child.

When La Toya walked into my office three years ago, she was finally able to lighten her load as a mom trying to provide everything she could for her son who lacked positive male role models. As for her son, he received a filler for the hole within his heart, affirming that he is a worthy young man, and there is nothing to stand in his way but himself. Well, his heart is partially complete because no man walking the earth could fulfill the space where a father's love and protection should exist.

In the book, when she begins to speak about her moment of truth and awakening concerning her manchild, you will want to be their propping posts. You'll want to stand beside her as she embarks with a focus embracing single motherhood, while standing tall on his behalf securing his stance. She does all of this as she takes him through the journey of being sure he does not become a statistic.

When most hear the coined phrases "baby mama" and "single mama," you can usually expect some father bashing to follow. Okay, granted sometimes it warranted, but that's not the point of this book. Ms. Grow is going to take you on a journey of transparency. You will feel her every emotion: her bitterness, moments of depression, revelations, growth, and triumphs. Trust me when I tell you that her passion explodes from each page!

I do hope moms will be able to find their voice through La Toya's story. This view will open you up to receive the breakthrough needed to power through life, with your children reaping the benefits. I also hope that fathers understand how vital their roles are in the lives of their children. Our young black men are already up against a wall in society, so why create more obstacles for them to hurdle? When relationships don't work, I hope this book encourages everyone to co-parent with the highest level of respect, to ensure your child rises each day knowing he or she is loved by all who matter. There is no chance in hell they will fail or become what society predicts!

Mr. L.C.Smith

Real Fathers Making a Difference, Inc.

Introduction

In my older age and growth, I have come to understand that the key problem with judging others is that you cannot dictate another person's experience. It is impossible for me to tell you what you went through and likewise. One can only make an observation and have an opinion based on what information they have regarding another's experience. This is the truth I have settled in as an adult whose aim is to do better as I become knowledgeable of what better is. This is why I cringe at the far-too-often generalization and negative attachment that is placed on single moms or should I say "baby mamas".

Yes, there are single moms who are difficult, negligent, disrespectful, and just outright poor representations of the title. Yes, there are black men who are consistently purposeful and impactful in their position of co-parent. Unfortunately for the latter, both are more so the "exception" than the "rule" when the phenomenon of "fatherless children" is surveyed and dissected. If this were not so, there would be no such thing as an *epidemic* of children being raised in one-parent households, that one parent predominantly being the mother. I would even be so bold to say that there are more single moms fighting for the functionality of their co-parenting situation than those that are perpetrating dysfunction.

Society's standards say that because he is being raised by me alone, my son is *more likely* to drop out of school, commit a crime, and end up in prison. This is aside from being a black male which forecast the same predictors and then some. Those standards also say that he is more likely to abandon his future offspring due to the generational curse "gifted" to him.

Raising My Manchild

Since I became a mom, my focus has been asserting all of my energy towards not being the stereotypical baby mama. In the face of all the disadvantages laid out before me, I would fight for us to win in life. This was my unspoken, subconscious promise to myself for the sake of my son. I've been diligent in my quest to be that exception. I am now at the part of my journey where I will add the agenda of negating the negative narrative attached to the title *Baby Mama*. This is my story. This is my way.

Chapter 1
The Disclaimer

"You may trod me in the very dirt but still like dust, I'll rise."
~Maya Angelou

Being a single mom can easily be compared to wearing the dreadful scarlet letter. From the time you become an unwed expectant mother, you are marked. You are stained; value depreciated. *You*, single mother, are the underdog. In religion, relationships, education, and in the workforce, you are a burden. In the wrestling match of life, the bet is rarely placed on you.

Well, now ain't that some bullshit? Yep, I thought so too! It's okay though. Despite what we may have been taught, good and bad are actually parallel. Because in everything bad, there is something good to be gotten from it. Whether or not you get it, well that's based on you. For me, I can confidently say that I have gained far more from being a single mom than I have lost, despite the negative stereotypes society would want to mark me with. Single motherhood has *made* me, so my truths are easily admitted. I know that some will not agree with some of the content in this book. Some will think, "the nerve of her to write a book!" This book is not for either group. This book is for every baby mama fighting to prove the predictions made by society regarding single moms and their children's outcome, less accurate. Also, for the single mom drowning in the solitude of

9

trying to do everything right for the sake of her child(ren), yet still being accused of being wrong and feeling as though she just can't win...this is for you.

Here are some disclaimers to "blow a kiss" at anyone looking to discredit my voice. For years, I allowed being a baby mama to cripple me with insecurities. I allowed my situation to cause me to lose sight of who I was and what great things I could accomplish. I am *not* that girl anymore.

Disclaimer #1: I am perfectly imperfect. I am aware that I have flaws and may have more that I have not yet become acquainted with. I have not made all of the right decisions through this journey and have not been short of mistakes. I have at times acted in haste and impulse and have allowed my emotions to get the best of me. Sometimes, I choose petty over mature and if provoked I am capable of rising to the occasion of being a full-out-bitch.

Disclaimer #2: I have few good things to say about the sperm donor ("donor" for short) and have no respect for him at all. Still, regardless of my personal feelings about him, I have always been an advocate for him and my son having a healthy relationship. More so, I am the pep squad for black men, so this is *not* a male bashing platform. This is simply my truth based on my experience in an attempt to give well-deserved light to us single moms who do everything they can to be the best moms they can be, yet still get negatively typed.

Disclaimer #3: This is neither a dissertation nor a devotion. I will at times use slang and break grammatical and conventional spelling rules if needed to get my point across. I may even use unladylike words, so prepare to clutch your pearls.

Now that I have gotten that out the way...

Chapter 2:
Bitter Beginnings

"As I walked out the door toward the gate that would lead to my freedom, I knew that if I didn't leave my bitterness and hatred behind, I'd still be in prison."
~Nelson Mandela

Every time I think about the nerve of the donor to ask me to have an abortion, to protect himself, and the fact that he had just disclosed to me that he in fact, already had another baby on the way; every time I think about when I was in labor and my best friend contacted him, his reply was "okay", followed by no visits or calls; Every time I think about the blatant disrespect and disregard, among many other occurrences...I remember the almost consuming bitterness. Yes, I was bitter! I not only own that fact about me, but I reserve the right to have been so. Though I can say that I no longer reside in that state of mind, it was a justifiable stop along the way.

The nasty B word" may be ugly and self-destructive, but it is a natural, emotional reaction to acts such as belittlement, disregard, and abandonment. I served my time in the exile of bitterness, and while it did rob me of time and headspace that cannot be bought back, it hardened me and gave me a shield; a shield I would come to need to combat the constant conflict. Trust me when I say being a baby mama is not for the faint at heart. Being bitter served its purpose...it gave me tough skin for the journey ahead.

Because I have sat in my own bitterness and have wrestled and toiled with it internally, I have a seat at the table among like-damaged vessels. I know firsthand the causes and the cure. That is why I have decided to speak up and speak out. If I can help it, no more will single moms inspired by these words, feel as though something is wrong with them for feeling the way they do.

The key to not becoming a victim to bitterness is working through it and choosing not to allow its consumption of you. What often makes this a hard feat is the fact that to us, bitterness has been made to be a sort of shameful plague. Therefore, we suppress it instead of working to remove it. If you are busy hiding a mess, how can you declutter? Exactly, you cannot! Healing begins and ends with standing in your truth. I did not know this at the time. Therefore, I allowed my bitterness to live within the walls of my apartment and begin to take root in my life. I was depressed and broken, unable to see any positive outcome for my situation. Here I was living in a city with no family, pregnant by an asshole who picked the worst time to reveal how awful of a person he was, surrounded by friends who were busy approaching graduation and relocation, and feeling abandoned and bitter. As a result, I isolated myself from my closest friends and family. I dropped out of school, not having any help with childcare. Then I consumed myself with trying to force a *boy* to play a role he was dead set against playing, who had teamed up with his other baby mama (ex-single mom might I add) who was also dead set against him playing the role of dad to a child other than hers. This, of course, led to constant bickering and total communication breakdown and blowups. The disrespect was ongoing. They could dish it, but trust me when I say I was a pro at reciprocation. Because you know, baby mama ain't no punk by a long shot! This is where my bitterness had landed me...STUCK up shit creek without a paddle.

I spent the first two years of my mothering journey crying more than my baby did. I was paralyzed with anger. How could he do this to ME? What had I ever done to him to make it so *easy* for him to hate me and commence to ruining my life? How could a human being equipped with a soul and conscience, completely disregard such a precious life that he helped to create? Oh, and the nerve of him to continue with his life as if not to skip a beat! See how this perspective is total victim? My bitterness was holding me hostage. It had power over me because I did not know how to combat it. I did not know how to combat it because I had not addressed my bitterness. Then again, who knew it was even an issue to address? After all, I had isolated myself from anyone who could have probably helped me through it, to be left alone with the shame of being just another bitter baby mama; a failure.

What finally helped me begin to overcome my bitterness was grace. That's really the only explanation I can give, the grace of God to shift my focus and choice. Over time, I had an epiphany. I had to choose my son. I had come to the realization that despite the noncustodial's negligence and abandonment, my baby son needed me to fight for him in a different, less dysfunctional way. The screaming matches and flamed insults were draining me emotionally and physically. That left less of me to be present for my son. He needed a mom who was emotionally together. Because his emotions were a direct result of mine. He needed my protection not just from a seemingly heartless sperm donor, but more importantly from a broken and bitter mother. This however, would prove to be yet another uphill battle in the fight of single motherhood. I also had to choose to be accountable for my own undoing in the situation. My ugly truth is that I was a willing participant in a "situationship" that I had no business being in from jump! I could argue that I was young and dumb and just did not know any better, but what does that change, really? I allowed my esteem and self-worth to be discounted for far too long, and the result of that led me down the path where I had found myself, dealing with the emotions I was struggling to deal with.

At any age, what is the reason we find ourselves having to grow through situations that cause us such internal detriment? For me personally, the culprit could be a number of variables. Maybe it was the fact that in my upbringing, I had no clear, positive example of what a healthy relationship between a girl and a guy or a woman and a man even looked like, until after I had already become a single mom. It could have also been the fact that my mother refused to talk to me about boys. Her approach to the birds and the bees was simply a no boys at all rule through middle school. By high school, I had gone to live with an older sister. Even then, there was no sound coming-of-age talk about relationships. So be it, there was no benchmark set for what expectations to have for the actions of a guy who had an interest in me. Like many adolescents, I learned about relationships via friends sharing stories and my own premature attempts to engage in the age-old boy meets girl experience.

I am no therapist, but I feel equipped enough to say that it is most likely a combination of all those factors, possibly others as well, that I have yet to unveil. While we know that identifying the reasons we find ourselves in certain situations does not change current realities, the accountability piece of acknowledging those reasons is necessary for the healing process. A big part of motherhood has been introducing myself to the parts of me that make me who I am, the parts of me I didn't know existed at the time of becoming a single mom.

If you have not confronted your anger at this point in your journey, I urge you to do it now. Let my story be a cautionary tale. Do not allow bitterness to rob you of the healing that awaits you. Once it gets a hold of you, it's a grip that has the capacity to paralyze your forward movement indefinitely. Why prolong the healing you are so deserving of? You and your child(ren) both deserve an emotionally healthy you. Yes, you absolutely have a right to be angry, bitter even. After all, you are a human being that has feelings and emotions. Despite the wrong decisions you made, you still did not deserve to be wronged in such a way. No one gets it as much as a fellow baby mama just trying to do better and be better. Still, do not get stuck in the abyss of all that is wrong in your situation. Instead, I challenge you to sit in it and find a way to work through it. It will drain you down to the core of your fiber, and it is a discomfort like none other. You will feel unstable at best, dealing with the varying degrees of emotion. Confronting your bitterness breaks you down. There is really no softer way to say it. It is only a part of the process though, to be beautifully pieced back together again. So hear me with your heart when I tell you that you are strong enough to face it. Face the brokenness, bitterness and whatever emotions you find yourself fighting to break free of, because there is so much more waiting for you on the other side of being stuck. No one gets to tell you that you have to stay stuck and broken, not even you.

Chapter 3:
Finding Peace

"Maturity is learning to walk away from people and situations that threaten your peace of mind, self-respect, values, morals or self-worth."
~Anonymous

"Girl, if I were you, I would…"

"Ooh, you are better than me!"

"Ain't no way!"

"Couldn't be me!"

"He got the right one, 'Cause I would…"

I have heard these phrases countless times, more in the earlier years of motherhood, but even still today. Listen, there are few worse feelings than feeling like a total punk and a spineless pushover. Especially, when you *know* your capability of being a hell storm. Let's face it; there are baby mamas whose primary intent is to be as difficult and problematic as possible towards their parental counterpart. They lack any regard for the necessity of the relationship between father and child. I have been intentional in not being that baby mama. However, that did not prevent the numerous accusations from the opposition.

My friends could not understand why I would not fight back in more action-based ways. Why was I not proving to them that I could be every bit of the bitch the donor and his partner-in-venom had tagged me? My friends knew me. I have never claimed to be free of offense in the situation. They knew of some of the early instances where I had counterattacked my parental counterparts with words of rage. They also knew that my personality has never positioned me as one to intimidate easily. Still, here I was choosing to bow out, to the best of my ability, to keep an already toxic existence from being worse.

It is hard to explain your actions to people who have never experienced what you are dealing with. We are all guilty in one way or another of predicting our own reactions based on our own perception of reality. The problem with that, if we ever find ourselves in a situation that tests us, rarely do we respond the way we predicted. Still often times, we are too quick to give our "if it were me" opinion, not realizing how it may weigh on a friend who is internalizing a battle of fighting to do the right thing. This is another reason why I isolated, along with the bitterness I dealt with.

Not all of my friends were questioning my restraint however. What has greatly sustained me in my journey as a single mother are those closest friends who remain my voices of wisdom, ration and my source of venting space. If we all take the time to thoughtfully assess our systems of support, I am sure we could pinpoint why God put each person in our life. In the case of my single mom journey, God gave me a best friend who overcame her own single mom journey before me and now has a husband who raises her daughter as his own. I watched her become a single mom, struggle and grow through her own journey, and ultimately rise above. She has led me by her example of standing firm and protective of her daughter, but always being fair and open within the conditions of her own story. She did right by her daughter and fought hard to co-parent despite opposing, and many times, offensive actions of her daughter's dad. Then God gave me a God-sister and counselor who, while she does not have kids of her own, was the product of a broken family where her dad decided that being with his family was no longer convenient for his path in life. The same feelings of abandonment, disregard and questionable worth my son has to learn to live with, she has endured into adulthood. She speaks to me in my darkest places of hurt and anger, reminding me that God is not dead and does in fact see and know all. She comforts my fears speaking to me, a scared mom, from a place of relation and parallel between her and my son. For me, she is the living representation that children also see and know. In due time, my son will possess a mature awareness of his dad's actions and his dad will be held accountable without me having to intervene. Also, God gives me the ministry of friends that I myself have to set the example for as a single mom and in some cases be a voice for the fatherless child of their significant other. I have come to understand that I am accountable for being a help to my close friends who have become single moms after me. It is my responsibility as a friend to encourage them and hold them high in low places along their journey, because no one knows quite like another single mother just how lonely it is to be the sole financial, physical, spiritual and emotional provider for a child...even in times when you do not feel like you have it in you to provide. I will tell any and everybody, "Being a single mom is not for the faint at heart." Therefore, it does matter whom you allow to be your influence. Your peace is a direct result of it.

The well-known African proverb tells us that it takes a village to raise a child. Who is in your village? What is your role among the tribe? These questions are important for you to know the answers to for a number of reasons. One to mention, it makes the journey less lonely and you see at least some of the purpose of it, sooner than later. Had I had an awareness, at the time, how much certain comments from my friends weighed on me, I could have confided in them and shared my perspective. Perhaps that would have caused them to be more conscious about their remarks. Instead, encouraging me more about the restraint I was showing. Then maybe instead of isolating when I felt bitter and lonely, I would have reached out more and found that they were indeed there to hold me up.

I am probably not the first person to tell you that what you are going through is not actually for you. We both know that I will not be the last, but it is worth the reminder. A life void of the knowledge of purpose is a quiet, sad story. The direction of your life should have everything to do with the purpose of it. With that being said, it serves you well to know that in your lifetime you will have many purposes, immediate and long term. I have learned that many of my purposes are tied to my motherhood journey in some way, you should know that also. It helps make the journey more bearable in those tough times. Had I failed myself along the way at any point, I would have no words of wisdom to minister to those friends who needed insight. Furthermore, this book would not be a tangible tool in which I could use to inspire many other single moms. Had I chosen a different way, who knows how it would have affected my son who is now happy for the most part, and in tune with his gifts and talents. He has been kept safe to grow and thrive.

Consider your influence and influences. Are you being watched, teaching those you are not even aware of? Are you being weighed down by the misguided actions of close friends? Know your village and know your role in the tribe. If you don't know it now, start seeking answers today. Those answers help define a portion of your purpose. From there, the journey seems less like a life of punishment and the load somehow seems lighter. Position yourself to get the full benefit of your village.

Chapter 4: The Release

"Wanna fly, you've got to give up the shit that weighs you down."
~Toni Morrison

I do not know exactly when it happened, but while searching for peace, I learned to fight. I mean, *forreal* fight. My thought process shifted and my mind changed. I no longer wanted to be the victim, the shame-filled baby mama, stuck and degreeless. Hopelessness no longer had a place in my headspace. I remember many nights, crying out to God in such desperation, asking that He do "it". I started to feel in my deepest self that where I was in life, the circumstance that surrounded me could not be all that God had for me. There had to be much more to life. Something in me could not settle with just continuing to get by and seeing myself only as a baby mama, working to pay bills. It was time for the pity party to be over and done with!

Somewhere deep down inside of myself, I knew I had to rise up; for the sake of my own hope and for the example I needed to set for my son. I would challenge even my own thinking! I was nobody's helpless, hopeless baby mama. I was a woman who had made some bad decisions, but would make good of it. I was a mother who needed to change my circumstances for the well-being of my son. I was self-reflecting and in need of myself to choose life over death. I reminded myself that I have never been weak. Life had not afforded me that luxury. While I have always been proud to be my mother's child, I had to no longer be my mother's child. Crazy, right? For me, the statement makes perfect sense. My mom raised me to be comfortably planted in my own strength, yes. She instilled morals and values that I have appreciated in value as I get older and wiser. However, my mom was a woman who lived in a constant state of financial stretch and lack. She often danced with worry as a single parent. As of high school, I had already surpassed her highest level of education and as her child up until her death, I never witnessed my mom exist in a functioning, loving and balanced relationship. Although she stood as a giant towering over all that she endured, her terms were not mine. I wanted a higher standard of living and I wanted a different reality for me and my son. The details he would one day tell of his mother would be different. Therefore, in pursuit of not being my mother's child in a negative way, but rather being my son's mom in a positive way, I had to figure some shit out...

I do not know if I had the awareness then, but I guess spiritually I had the revelation that I had to take my power back. I had spent too much time focusing on everything that was against me winning at life. My circumstances and mentality had become my own personal imprisonment. I thank God for the "but" of that season though. I was a struggling, no-degree having, low-income living, minimum-wage earning baby mama, BUT I was at the dawn of my breakthrough. I realized that my breakthrough was in my break out! No, it did not all happen in an instant. Change is not static, it is continuous. Still, my decision to ignite my power and move past my paralysis had been made. My release from the dramatic existence of baby mama drama had activated. I could no longer afford to be held, bound by the worry of getting even or by keeping up with my son's father. The mental, spiritual and emotional well-being of my son and myself required me to "unpack my bags" and start my journey of moving on.

Here is where I talk to you in my "teacher voice". You can do this the easy way or the hard way. It is your choice. Either way, you are going to learn to fly TODAY (refer back to the quote at the start of this chapter)!

In my third grade classroom, I make it a habit to be intentional about sharing some of my imperfections with my students. I do it because I believe there is much value in exposing them to the human side of their teacher. This indirectly teaches them that adults make mistakes too, teachers can also learn new things from students, and it is okay to not know everything. I firmly believe by doing so, I validate them as individuals and create a safe space for them to make mistakes and still not fear trying. This way we become partners in their learning.

My Intentions placed on this body of work is that my words validate you not only as a single mom but also as an individual that is learning and growing through your journey. I have certainly made mistakes along my motherhood journey and I do not pretend to be perfect within these pages. Know that I am just like you. There is a lot that I did not know along the way and I am learning more about being a mother as the days pass. Still, I am sure of what I have written on these pages. I am so sure of you and me. We are not what society thinks of us just because we are raising our sons and daughters primarily on our own. We are also not the lies that have been told of us by the non custodial, who have at times sought to defame us. Instead, we are partners in our healing. Showing up for ourselves and doing the work to rise to our best selves. We are...MOTHERS. Those three words carry so much strength!

At this moment, I challenge you to survey your mindset. If there are any thoughts of belittlement or self-doubt lingering, I charge you to put in the work to dismantle them. If it takes reaffirming yourself ten times a day, do it. Do it until it is embedded in your being. Do it until you start to feel yourself grow wings. Why? Because, you need them to fly.

Chapter 5:
Moving Forward

"The past is a place of reference, not a place of residence."
~ Roy T. Bennett

So, I'm ready. It's GO-time! My mindset is better because I have been praying about it. I've even worshipped at the altar over it. Plus, I have sprinkled in a few fasts over it. I mean, I am serious and armed with all the positive outlook I can contain. I mean business! My vision board is done and posted up, because of course you are not truly serious about changing the course of your life if there is no vision board involved. Life would surely be better now that my mind was made up about wanting more out of life and I somewhat had a plan for bettering my circumstances. I would reenroll in school while working and get my degree, so I could start my career and be able to afford a more comfortable standard of living. Things would be just fine. My life's plan may have been stalled by *my* bad decisions, but it was certainly not ruined. I could turn things around, knowing that what the devil meant for evil, God would use for my good. Here goes...I'm taking one step with FULL expectation that God will take two. I am AMPED! MOVITATED! PUMPED! On the mark, get ready, get set...

I'll—be—damned! Life as a baby mama, struggling to make ends meet, gave no cares about me making the decision to get my life together. Who would have thought it? There was no sudden set change or plot twist that fell out of the sky at the moment of my life-changing epiphany. In fact, years would pass and I was seemingly stuck in what felt like a recurring nightmare where things would always look as if I was about to reach a new level of accomplishment, only to knock me back down to my reality every single time. If it was not one thing, it was three more things to remind me that I remained bound to my situation. From one low-paying job to another, typically having to quit before being fired, because I could not consistently pay for childcare. I got back in school only to end up quitting again because I could not afford the payment plan option I elected at the time of enrollment. Why was this even a realistic option to me anyway? I guess the only rational logic is that I just wanted to try, by any means necessary. If I can give myself any credit at this season in my life, I have to acknowledge that I kept pedaling at the wheel despite my ignorance of approaches. For example, finances aside, how was I going to be a full-time student, when my greater need for survival was being a full-time employee? That scenario is easily possible for a young mom living in close proximity to family and close friends. However, That was not my situation. My closest friends either graduated or married and moved away shortly after my pregnancy and birth, and I had no relatives in the city. It wasn't until my son was one year old that I began to nurture relationships within my church family, many of whom eventually became my most substantial support system as a single mom.

Being discouraged and disappointed had become what was normal for me. When I was not in between jobs, I was in between living on my own or having to live with one of my church families. When I was living on my own, some months seemed as if I was finally catching my breath in life, other months I was borrowing money to get my utilities reconnected, buy food, pay daycare or get gas. A constant cycle of "robbing Peter to pay Paul". You are probably thinking, "What about child support",right? Well, I'm sure you can guess how that played out. I was literally trying to survive solely off of my minimum wage income and no consistent help at all from the donor. Other outside financial sources included my older brother and sister, my then pastor, and a couple of great friends on occasion. For several years, despite having a child support order, I saw no financial assistance from the donor at all. Eventually, child support did start to come out of his check and I was able to rely on those funds. It helped me sustain for a short period. Yet as the story often goes, that lasted only until he changed jobs. Then I would see checks, it seemed, whenever it was convenient for him to pay. Times when payments would stop for months at a time, I would assume he had "better" things to do with his money, like show up at our prestigious alma mater for homecoming, or take trips and buy nice things to post about it on social media.

The biggest lesson of it all was learning to make it my business to get at least financially stable enough that I did not have to rely on his money. After all, as a mom and the custodial parent, it is my primary responsibility to provide for my son. If no one else decides to do anything for him, it is my job to see to it that my son does not go without. Who has time for sitting around crying, complaining and making excuses, when I had a child to raise, protect and provide for? Not any *good* mother. Good mothers find a way. Good mothers figure out the details of life as they go through it, refusing to stop because their child(ren) depend on them. Above all else, I was determined to be a good mother. By any means necessary, I would leave the excuses behind and work towards creating stability for my son and myself. I would be a good mother.

You too are a good mother. Despite what the naysayers in your life may want others to believe, you are thriving through motherhood. If you were not, you would not have cared to read this book, but here you are. So if there is any doubt in your mind about being a good mother, let me affirm you in this space. I hope that the good days of your journey grossly outweigh the bad days. When the bad days seem worse, my prayer is that you can find solace within these pages, many times after the first read.

Biblical beliefs teach that man cannot live by bread alone. If you believe that, then you know how important it is to digest what makes us whole and spit out what may eat away at our insides. With that in mind, I challenge you to swallow these words. Then chase them with affirmations of your own, with the understanding that what you put out into the universe will return to you. Speak to those dreams you had to put on hold when motherhood showed up and to the financial stability you want to have for you and your child(ren). Give everything that you want for yourself permission to show up.

Things do not just get better, simply because we changed our mind. Your ability to redirect your perspective along the way is major. When things just aren't sorting out, it is so easy to get lost in a downward spiral of emotions. The bills, deferred dreams, issues with your kid(s), the conflict with the donor, and I am sure the list could continue; can all make it hard to remain hopeful and positive. You get to an emotional halt where you can't see the forest for the trees. The details of your circumstance cloud your ability to press on. This is the place where you must dig deep down and pull out that undefeated fight and resilience that all of us mothers possess. You may not even realize that about yourself yet, but I promise you it is there.

Changing our perspective about how lack shows up in our life is a gamechanger. Our perception is our reality. You will have to learn to intentionally look at the glass half full. It takes a lot of practicing and unlearning habitual processing, but it is necessary. That is the only way you can truly overcome being stuck dealing with the shadow of lack. Instead of focusing on the unpaid child support for the month, redirect the focus towards the checklist of bills that were still able to be paid with what money you had. Instead of focusing on the fact that you may be temporarily having to live with someone until you get back on your feet, maybe even for the second or third time, focus on the fact thankfully you have someone in your life willing to take you and your child(ren) in. There are single moms whose testimony if not of living with friends or family members, but of living in their car or between shelters. The point is there is also light to be found in darkness. When we put more energy towards acknowledging what we do have over what we lack in our circumstances, it makes what we don't have less pronounced in our lives. It also makes it easier for us to start to build a life of stability for us and our children.

Chapter 6:
Purposeful Healing

"One of the most important relationships we have is the relationship we have with our mothers."
~Iyanla Vanzant

As Mother Iyanla Vanzant has continued to teach us, healing is a very necessary process for the legacy of our descendants, which requires great work. I do not ever want my emotional burdens to end up in my son's lap when he himself becomes an adult. Therefore, I have had to be intentional about my journey toward healing and forgiveness. I am not fully there yet, and I make no apology for that truth. It is a process that only God and I can govern. I am okay in this space and to anyone who would feel compelled to judge me; to them I would say, "Fuck you and the high horse you rode in on." What bothers me more than anything is when a person who thinks they know your situation is so quick to pass judgement on you if you even act like you want to show an emotional reaction about some bullshit the donor has done. People kill me taking the position that baby mamas have no right to be humans with feelings. This holds especially true in the social media age we exist in. Those who know me know that I do have a discipline to keep my business off of social media. It is simply not the platform to air out your dirty laundry. Even with young children who may not be of age to facilitate social media pages, no rational thinking mom wants to be an embarrassment to her child(ren).

Posting out of impulse and emotion could also cause more conflict between counterparts. What benefit is that to the child(ren) involved? These are just some of the things I have told myself or my more reasonable thinking friend has told me to refrain from acting out in a fit of temper. As a good mom whose heart is truly for the wellbeing of my son, I can usually count on his best interest to center me. However, there have been times when I wanted to post every detail of dirt to debunk the façade of the donor, I have dealt with for years now. The fact that I have managed to show restraint over the years in that degree, counts as an emotional win in my book. Still, although not to that degree, there have been times over the years where I used social media as an outlet to make general statements that absolutely derived from what I had been dealing with in my personal situation. Because this is my emotional journey that I am working through on my terms, I believe it is fair that I reserve the right to choose how I deal; so does any single mom who is fighting to maintain sanity while healing and growing. Growth, maturity and healing are all processes. Processes take time, and in some cases, take reevaluating and remapping before getting it right. What is important is that we moms know that the process of healing is necessary, because our inability to process trauma of any kind directly affects our children.

Every day is not going to be a day of emotional wins as a single mom. Some days your life will feel stable and peaceful, other days you will feel the full bluntness of your reality. It is not always easy to remain positive and recognize the wins of each day when you are the head of household, teacher, preacher, counselor, disciplinary, manager and supervisor to your child. Some days the only win is that you did not give up. Allow me to reassure you that is okay! Society would have us believe that our strength is in holding all of life pieces together despite our circumstances. I would defiantly rebuttal that by saying our true strength is simply in fighting through falling apart and reassembling the pieces as many times as necessary to keep going. Give yourself permission to not have it all together at times. No one has it *all* together! I cannot count the many times I have had to hide from my son to have a complete come-apart. Sometimes it was in the tub with worship music playing and candles lit, other times it was in bed at night after he had gone to sleep. Then there were those times when the unravelling would happen completely unannounced and I would find myself mid-breakdown while he played in the next room or watched TV. I rarely told more than two people I trusted about those moments because I did not want to appear weak and broken. I wanted those closest to me to think that I was successfully figuring life out and for them to be proud of me. I had no baby-mama Fairy God Mother telling me to just breathe through it and accept the human essence, the feminine strength of those breakdowns. So here I am telling you. You do not owe anyone an apology for being human first, not even yourself. To be left holding the great responsibility of parenthood alone is a grave trauma. You will not heal overnight nor will you walk in forgiveness immediately. You will overcome it all though. There is strength embedded in your womanhood. Single motherhood is simply a battle from which you are earning your stripes. Those many breakdowns are your heart's war cry. Whether you believe it or not, they revive your will to continue on. They recharge your inner strength to define your own victory for yourself and your child(ren). Press on...

The hardest part of the journey, by far, is submitting to true healing. Honey, when I tell you it is a journey within itself, I mean it! There is nothing neat and pretty about soul work, especially when you are confronting trauma. It was not until recently that I gained the understanding that healing begins and ends with you. Are you ready to confront yourself? If you are still struggling with stiffening anger, you have not started healing. For the sake of your child(dren), you have a decision to make here and now.

Taking personal inventory in the process of sorting out soul damage is flat out uncomfortable. Five years ago, I don't know if I had the ability or awareness even, to publicly admit that I have a child by a person I was in a "situationship" with, whom I had no business being with because nothing about the experience was worth risking aids and other STDs for. Because really, to lay with a dog and not get up with fleas is God's grace. Instead, I was blessed with this beautifully complicated being. I have the pleasure of him calling me mom. Could you be blunt about your own situation in the manner you just read about mine? Accountability cannot wait on the other person. It shows up to the party with you. The ugly truth is, you and I both would not be someone's baby mama had we made different decisions. Still, that does not mean we deserve the treatment we have been recipients of. It also does not mean that society's judgement of us is accurate or just. However, it does mean that our circumstances started with us. Therefore, it will take us confronting our own part in order to come out.

The good news is that once you have slayed your own demons, there is no judgement strong enough to make you feel the shame and belittlement you once carried with the title Baby Mama. You are released from the opposing viewpoint which frees you to operate with the tunnel vision of what's best for you and your child(ren).

Chapter 7:

An Unpopular Truth

"Cause ain't nothing worse than when your son wants to know
why his daddy don't love him no more."
~Tupac Shakur

The hardest part of my own journey of healing through single motherhood has been the anxious anticipation that one day, I will no longer feel so compelled to protect my son from being hurt and disappointed by his dad, because he will have his own awareness within our reality of his absentee father. Several times, I have had both my best friend and God sister tell me not to worry about all the things the donor does or does not do, because one day my son will see it for himself. He will form his own opinion about the absenteeism of his father. Just give it time... "When? How long will that take? How much emotional damage will be done to my son in the meantime?" I am well aware that no one knows the answers to these questions but God. That still does not stop me from screaming them out at times. I naturally want to guard my son's heart as much as possible and it more than pisses me off when I am treated as if I am being difficult or conflicting, in moments when I am only protecting his emotional state. It is hard, because as a mom, my first and second instincts are to nurture and protect. No parent ever wants to feel like they have failed their child(ren) in any way. To see him hurting, knowing

I cannot fix the offense leaves me feeling helpless. I do not ever want to be helpless when it comes to my child. I want to be his earthly refuge whenever he is experiencing chaos or unrest in his world. So yes, I initially fought and fought hard for the relationship between my son and his father because I knew without it, my son would have holes in his upbringing. I wanted a functional, emotionally safe relationship though. Therein lied the problem!

They (the donor and his counterpart) wanted me to "shut up and sit down" so to speak. Thinking they could just handle me as disrespectful as they may and I was supposed to be the good baby mama and stay in line. In the words of a good friend, "I'm straight, I'll die!", said sarcastically of course. This statement means I would take death as an option before complying. I am not a shut up and sit down type of girl; neither am I a girl who will agree to talk solely to and through the then girlfriend now wife of my child's father, when it concerns the child that I did not have with her. Especially when you consider our very first encounter was her taking over a phone conversation between he and I, and her having the audacity (as a single mom at the time herself), to tell me that he would do nothing for my son before taking care of her kids. It was that action that cancelled any possibility of me ever having any respect for her as a mom and woman. As history would have it, from that moment on she too would be my arch nemesis as long as she held the arrogant position that my son was less worthy of care than her kids were. Although the exact words of him being less have never come out of her mouth, especially not to my ears, her actions said it all. From the very beginning, the excuses ranged from "you just want him (the donor)", "you just want to cause conflict in our household" from her, to him accusing "I can't have a relationship with my son because you are difficult to deal with". It was ALWAYS me. Despite my countless efforts to make it easy for the donor to be a dad to his *other* child, I was always the scapegoat for both him and his sidekick. So then, if being a scapegoat is what I have to be to protect the emotional state of my son, that is exactly what I will be, happily. The donor does not get to be a half ass dad that doesn't make contact for months and years at a time, disregard my son's whole existence, provide not a dime more than the inconsistent child support payments, yet expect me to just shut up and sit down. All of which is just breaking the surface of the neglect done to my son.

Imagine if you will, a man who is well-educated, gainfully employed, family oriented, a well-traveled educator, school counselor, entrepreneur, author and youth motivator. He has made a career based on his passion of creativity and encouraging youth. He travels near and far to motivate schools of children and adults, he mentors young men and he prides himself on valuing family and being a dad to his *two* children, whom he proudly posts on his social media platforms expressing his love and pride towards them. I should mention that one of those children is a stepchild unlike my son who is organically his offspring. I firmly believe he is right to love her as his own. I just do not understand how he has the moral compass to treat her as his own, yet utterly disregard his actual flesh and blood. However, I digress on that point.

This guy has multiple retail products including t-shirts, wristbands and books. One of his books is titled *Breaking Generational Curses*... HA! How is that for hypocrisy? Hypocrisy yes, because while his two kids have shirts, books, wristbands and bragging rights to accompany their dad's accomplishments and their relationship with him, my son does not have SHIT from this man. My son has not been afforded the opportunity to be proud of his dad nor has he been privileged to experience being tagged in a loving post on any one of his dad's social media pages. Hell, he has not even had a happy birthday phone call, ever, from his dad, not on the actual date! I can tell you of two times for sure, he has even asked my son to remind him of the date of his birthday. His birthday is on St. Patrick's Day. Granted, it is not a black holiday. However, you have to put forth a lot of effort into forgetting that your child was born on any holiday.

Also, this man is in our city on a regular basis throughout the year thanks to his wife's family being here as well our alma mater. Yet, I can count on one hand how many times he has called to see his son while visiting. Oh yeah, that is right...it is because I am too difficult to deal with. Well, for years I have been calling bullshit on that. Imagine knowing your child has not heard from his dad in months and has not seen him in over a year or two. Then you hear that he is in town visiting, by word of mouth versus him contacting you to see his kid. How would you feel? Unfortunately still, despite the many years that have passed, the bullshit has not. He continues to lay the foundation for a paternal generational curse that my black son does not deserve to have handed down to him.

So then, what do I tell my son? What do you tell your child(ren) when they want to know why they are not *good enough* to be loved by their dad? My son is now at the age where he is now becoming emotionally mature enough to see for himself what is wrong with him and his dad's nonexistent relationship. I provide emotional support and counsel in moments where I see fit. However, it has always been extremely important to me to protect his emotional wellbeing while establishing an honest space surrounding the circumstances concerning his dad.

There have been and will always be many debates about what you should or should not say to or around your child about their negligent dad. Overall, a position that is often presented is that despite the circumstances, no mom should ever down-talk a child's dad to or around them. I do absolutely agree with this position. However, what definitions of down-talk apply to the statement? For me, I refuse to set a false pretense of what love looks and feels like for my son, for the sake of not down-talking his dad. Why? Because I am raising a black man who will have his own inherited hurdles to overcome throughout his life. I feel it would be doing him a major disservice to not teach him what real love is, feels and acts like. Nothing in me desires to have my son grow up and have the same character flaws as his dad, or myself even, but definitely not his dad as a man and father. I want my black son to grow up to be an adult who is emotionally stable, safe and fulfilled. I want him to know that love will only manifest itself in healthy conditions. Love does not take anything away from your esteem, it only gives and builds. While I will not ever be so insensitive to tell my son that his dad does not love him, I make no apology for telling him that the abandonment and disregard his dad has handled him with are not actions of love. It is my priority and duty to see to it that when he himself is an adult, he has an established benchmark for those who claim to love him and he has a moral compass for his own actions towards those he loves. So, while I have not viciously dragged his dad for his ear to hear, I have had some very authentic, careful but honest conversations about his dad with him. I have made factual statements in front of him about his dad that did not cast a positive light. I have let my authentic emotions show in times of frustration and disappointment, even anger. I do not apologize for it and refuse to let anyone tell me that I am wrong in doing so. If it is all I can do to guide him on his way towards manhood and fatherhood, he will know that the disregard his dad has shown towards him is not the norm nor is it the standard for love.

I am now and will always be of the belief that it is absurd to protect the image of a man who has proven to have no compassion nor care towards his own child, for the sake of my son eventually figuring it out on his own. While I am also of the belief that it is equally absurd for me as a mom who wants what is best for my son emotionally, to add toxicity to the matter. Balance and compassion are always significant. I am well aware that there has to be a degree of boundary and level of empathy in the way I manage my son regarding him and his dad. As he has gotten older, the attempts have become easier.

There are few things harder in this world than consoling your young man-child who is crying and longing for a relationship with his dad. Despite your total disgust and embedded bitterness, you still find the strength to reassure your son that his dad *does* love him although he is choosing not to have a relationship with him. Having to offer reassurance that you yourself do not have on even your most gullible days is indeed a mom's super power. Yet, through the tears you cry along with and for your son, you make it believable enough to comfort him and offer him hope that maybe one day, by prayer, God will change their situation, and he will have the time and engagement he longed to have with his dad. *This* is what we single moms do best. We find strength where there is seemingly none to be found, in order to be the super hero our child(ren) need.

That was a rough period for both my son and myself. That helpless feeling I talked about, that no parent ever wants to experience, I soaked in it because that was what my son needed from me in that season. However, as I found strength to console my son with the assurance of his dad's invisible love, I recycled anger and bitterness towards his dad. Why was I angry? Why was my bitterness rising back up? The answer for me is because that was still an example of protecting the image of his dad who outright did not deserve it. I hated to be the one to have to do that *to* my son. I owed that deadbeat no protection! Protection was supposed to be reserved for my son. So, as he has gotten older, it has been my duty to protect his emotional development to the height of my emotional ability, as we both continue to grow and heal.

I definitely understand the context of the saying, "the road to hell is paved with good intentions". I understand that just because you mean well, does not mean your actions will not have detrimental consequences. Yes, you should always be open to correction and enlightenment when it comes to growing through your motherhood journey. Wisdom has an immeasurable value. However, do not be afraid to stand for what you know is right, as it concerns your child(ren). God chose you for the ultimate responsibility of raising a human. That is such a loaded duty within itself. I do not think there is a mother alive who does not at the very least want to produce a good person into the world. So then, what factors into the makeup of a good person? What life experiences alter the likelihood or degree of good in a person? As you ponder the answer to these questions, do so considering that the mom figure in a person's life is the gatekeeper to their "ingredients of good". Now, with that perspective, does it not make sense that you would do everything in your power to protect the emotional wellbeing of your child? Keep fighting mama! Just remember to balance the protection with honesty.

I am sure we could sit and trade "war" stories about the people we have conceived with, for hours on end, and that would be completely okay and even helpful to us. However, sometimes we need to get out of our raw emotions to make way for reason. Sometimes talking through upsetting situations is an act likened to counting to ten. You know, like the classic anger management tactic of counting as a way to avoid an irrational action. What helped me have the strength to hold my son and tell him that his dad loved him and that one day they would have the relationship he longed for, was having safe spaces where I could verbally assault the donor and express the depth of my anger. It was like taking the longest deep breath after being held under water long past my comfort level. These instances were literally an emotional re-centering, and I am so appreciative of the few close friends who allowed me to have these moments free of judgement. There is definite power in numbers. By myself, I probably didn't have the restraint to show up for my son in many of the ways I have mentioned. When he cried to me, the flawed human I am probably would have told him "too bad, your dad doesn't love you. Suck it up". Thankfully, I had people who allowed me to lean on them, giving way for me to access that mama strength I have also mentioned. If you haven't accessed your mama strength and have found yourself compromising the emotional wellbeing of your child(ren), hit the reset button right now. Apologize to them for the damage that has been done, then make the decision to do better as you now know better. Doing better may start with identifying what people in your life provide a safe place for you as a mom. Start there. Again, just remember to balance the protection with honesty. Honesty is okay. It is necessary, but the delivery of honesty does matter.

Chapter 8:

Planting Mustard Seeds

"Not everything faced can change, but nothing can be changed until it is faced."
~ James Baldwin

As a mom of a brown boy, I carry a number of fears that I feel are both valid and rational. At the top of the list, I do not want him to grow up having hidden all of his pain and having turned to a life of drugs and/or crime as a source of coping. Nor do I want him to grow up with so much resentment for his dad that he grows to hate him, and that hate manifests in the form of him also being a deadbeat to his offspring. Likewise, I do not want him to grow up with resentment towards me because of the protection I chose to shield him with in relation to him and his dad. I also do not want him to grow into a person of bad character, because history has shown us that hurt people hurt people.

One of the many life lessons I remember from my mother's wealth of wisdom is that problems do not just disappear (if unresolved) they only fester. Therefore, I want him to feel safe in spaces of sorting through his broken pieces as he decides the man he will be in this life. I want his childhood to be his testimony for all the great things he will do, instead of his excuses for all the bad decisions I hope he never has to make. So,

41

what do I do to silence my fears? How do I fight to continue to bring those thoughts under subjection? What help is there for a single mom who simply wants her brown boy to develop into a whole individual?

At first, searching for help in rearing a man-child was just another discouraging disappointment. Again, I am in a city with no family. Therefore, there are no uncles or big cousins to come scoop Jaden up to go watch a game or grab a bite to eat, just to get a break from constantly being around females. My closest brother lives in Florida and closest brother-in-law, in Georgia. While Jaden adored them early on, the distance just does not allow the male influence needed on a day-to-day, in depth basis. There were also no relationships that became serious enough for me to trust him bonding with a boyfriend either. I firmly believed in and abided by the responsible single mama "rule" that you don't expose your child(ren) to every Tom, Dick and Harry you meet! I did not want my son burdened with the trauma of having extra "uncles" and mama's "friends" who too would eventually leave, creating deeper abandonment scars for us both. So I kept the woman side of me largely separated from the mama side. Of course, you can never truly disconnect from being a single mom and that fact alone carries its own burden on relationships, but that is another book to be written... Still, I knew I needed help, but having the right help was pivotal. Raising a black man does not afford you too many errors to be made. I had to get it right if I were to get any help at all.

First, I tried sports. I mean, it is the natural course of action when raising a boy right? The only problem was that my boy held zero interest in sports. He was and is an art-driven creative. We tried it anyway. The goal was to get him exposed to positive male models and engaged with more male peers. Sports were an obvious solution for both. However, He hated football. He played for two years and did give it an A-grade effort, but it was not the answer. He made no connection to the coaches or the boys because simply put, he was different. A fish out of water is the best description for him and sports. I had to figure out another avenue to bridge the gap of male influence. So then came the search for mentor programs. Being in a college "town" there are plenty. From the Greek Letter Organizations, churches, to community groups, they exist by the dozens. You would think it would have been an easy find..Wrong! I quickly learned that the great need for male mentors is largely unbalanced over the actual number of male mentors. That was not the only problem. Many of the programs I found were what I often call surface-leveled; generic would be a more befitting term. There is too much at stake for us single moms to give our sons over to programs that put in minimal time with a few activities spread out over time with no real substance or consistent guidance. Wearing bow ties and suits is a real good look for young men, but my son's dad has taught me the life-long lesson that even if you dress shit up with a fancy, big polished bow it still smells and is disgusting, because it is still in fact shit. I needed someone who would climb in the trenches alongside me and literally operate in the voided space of the absentee donor. The fight I am in is multidimensional. There are levels to this "thang"! A tall order for the greatest of champions... That is a commitment in which I'm aware that many are not equipped or positioned to make. Yet, God saw my need. He knew the fears of my heart well before I became a mom. He also knew that He had a solution all along. What I didn't know was that parallel to the years of my struggles through single motherhood, Real Fathers Making A Difference, Inc. would be building and growing, waiting to cross paths with me and my man-child.

It is often said that "knowing is half the battle". I believe most single moms know and agree with the fact that women cannot teach boys how to be men. If you disagree, try to follow my explanation. In the classroom, the best teachers are always the ones who have to ability to connect their content knowledge with real-world application. Otherwise, you are simply an information provider and retention of the information is less likely. When we have experienced things ourselves, we teach from a different perspective. First person perspective is more detailed than third person perspective. The more details you can give a student about a topic, the better they are able to activate their ability to visualize, which is a comprehension strategy. This is why teachers prepare for lessons. We want to equip ourselves with enough information to teach content from a first person experience, with the objective that we provide students with enough details for them to comprehend. With that analogy in mind, think of men as teachers who are naturally prepared to teach young boys about manhood. From puberty to pop culture, our female lens can in no way see all the details of growing from boyhood to manhood. We need a man for that!

Chapter 9:
Harvest

"It is easier to build strong children than to repair broken men."
~ Fredrick Douglass

I had a chance encounter via social media with a mom from the program. I met her during a Christmas giveaway I had collaborated in; in the name of my grassroots nonprofit I was starting called Manchild, Inc. Manchild would be a financial resource for moms of boys who lacked the finances to pay for extracurricular activities for their sons. The idea for my nonprofit came about after my own experience of wanting to enroll my son in some type of extracurricular activity that would put him around positive male influences. I could not afford the expense on my own and when I, against better judgement, asked my son's dad for financial assistance, he shot me down. He directed me to use the monthly child support that he inconsistently paid for any expenses concerning our son. For fifteen years now, his payments have been the same amount, three hundred seventy-five dollars. At the time, I was paying for before and after school care. That amount didn't even cover that monthly expense alone. Thankfully, I had the support of close friends and my few faithful family members. The donor's ex best friend, a mutual friend of ours, gave me the one hundred fifty dollars I needed to put my son in football and my God-sister helped me with practice apparel. It was my awareness that not all single moms had such a support system, which drove the purpose of Manchild, Inc. Participating in the Christmas giveaway would be one of my first initiatives as an established nonprofit.

In speaking with the mom through messenger, I found out about Real Fathers Making A Difference (R Fathers M.A.D.), Inc. She spoke so highly of the program that had been a great help to her and her boys. The conversation was an equal exchange of encouragement from one mom to another. The exchange ended with her giving me the telephone number to R Fathers M.A.D.'s office. I wasted no time calling, only to find out that there was a waitlist and the wait could be a year or more. I could not help but revisit the disappointment I had come to know so well. She spoke with such regard for the program; I could not help but have an immediate excitement. This was it. This was just what I needed. Therefore, I would wait.

Because sometimes things just have a way of working out, my wait ended up being less than six months. It turned out a number of boys graduated from school and the program that May. That opened up enough spots that reached my son on the waitlist. Therefore, the next school year, he would start the program. It is this type of grace that reminds me that God is not dead within my journey.

The intake interview was short and blunt. Still, I left with embedded hope deep down in my spirit. The director was straightforward and firm, and his passion for *his* boys was evident even sitting across the desk, meeting him for the first time. His disposition as he spoke showed ownership and accountability for the boys in his program. I do not know if it makes sense to say, but it was one sole act, outside of all the information provided that day, that confirmed my confidence in the program. He regarded my son, validated him as a young man and that was everything to me. Immediately, trust was established for both my son and I. How, you ask? A simple act of asking direct questions as my son and I sat together, then excusing me and allowing my son to speak freely without the conviction of his mom. It made sense to me and convinced me that he knew what my son needed as a boy who would grow into a man. It was there that our partnership began.

That day has now been over three years ago. Since then I have watched my son find his way through his own metamorphosis, making his way toward manhood. It has not been without incident. Raising a teenager has been a hazing of sorts. My son is a great kid, but he is a great kid without a father who lacks academic and occasional practical motivation, and in transparency, who has been sheltered by his mom. The reality is and will always be that my gender and my protectiveness sometimes hinders the process of shaping the man I am raising.

R Fathers M.A.D. has been my co-parent in every sense of the word. Talks about hygiene, porn, internet predators and college readiness are only a scratch on the surface of the depth of parenting the mentors of the program have provided, far past presentations and field trips. I have been a direct benefactor of the fullness of this program and my gratitude will remain imprinted in the fabric of my single mom journey.

You need help. Trust me, it is not as helpless a statement as it sounds. It is okay to need help and to accept it. I have learned that. Not just as it concerns finding a mentoring program to enroll my brown boy in, but in motherhood period. Maybe it has something to do with having been abandoned with the mountainous responsibility of raising another human being alone, but I think within that space, we develop certain complexes as individuals. One being the need to prove that we are actually strong enough to do it. At least for me, because this one person theoretically said "do it by yourself!" my fight-or-flight response was "damn right, I will!" The challenge is on. The question we have to ask ourselves though is, "Is my purpose to prove them wrong, having a successful motherhood journey as a byproduct, or is my purpose in this (journey) to be a successful mom?"

You are justified in wanting to prove everyone who has ever doubted you wrong from the moment God blessed you with life growing inside your womb. Especially the one person who has impaled your self-esteem, leaving you not only with a wound to self-treat, but also with the emotional, mental and financial debt of motherhood. However, I charge you to see past the hurt of the circumstance that brought you to motherhood, and instead embrace the grace of what will become of you because of motherhood. I promise, you will be better because of everything you are going through as you raise your child(ren). Remain grounded in the fight within yourself, but be strong and wise enough to know that the true way you win at single motherhood is by doing what is best for your child first. This journey of life is not designed to travel alone, the same holds true for motherhood. We as women cannot give a male child the things he needs to be a man. We can only attribute to the value and integrity of his character as a human being. This does not discount us as the most important factor in our child's upbringing, it only sets precedence for the chosen strategy. Find the right help and keep it! What one man will not do another man will. That is your power play and has the potential to be a chess move. Like the game of life, motherhood is a game of chess not checkers. We want to set our children up to win.

Chapter 10:
This too Shall Pass

"Sometimes you've got to lose to win again."
~Fantasia

Mentorship definitely has its place in single parenthood. My son Jaden and I have reaped many benefits in the years he has been in R. Fathers M.A.D. He has matured greatly overall and I have been less overwhelmed in some areas. Because of our experience, I will always advocate for mentorship for children who are being raised by a single parent. It just makes sense. When you find a program that works for your situation, it is truly a godsend. Still, mentorship as great as it is, was also not a "fix-a-flat" for my single mom journey either.

I can explicitly remember the *many* moments of wishing for a man, just plainly put. Of course, as a natural woman my desire for a man is primarily for companionship and love. With that, I would be lying if I said I didn't want a man to be my partner in parenting almost equally. Far before I became a single mom, I have always desired having my own family consisting of a husband, kids and myself. After becoming a single mom, raising a manchild, I on some days *desperately* longed to have a man as my partner helping me to raise my son and helping me to stand up against the bullies I had to try to co-parent with. This is not to say that I was desperate for a man though. Please acknowledge the difference. I feel no shame in saying that I wanted my brown boy to grow up having a direct example of black love. I wanted him to see his mom being loved and coexisting in a functional relationship. I wanted to be included in the list of relationships he would model his after in his adult years.

As much as I admire and respect my parents, they were not the ideal or even the most decent example of black love. My mom married in her early twenties to the dad of four of my older siblings. It wasn't until her death that I found out that they never actually legally divorced. I can only assume that somewhere along her journey she decided remarrying wasn't a reality or possibly even a desire for her. The relationship with my dad was one of the last relationships of her lifetime. They spent years together, presumably in love at least part of the time, but unable to be the mate that they each apparently needed to elevate each other respectfully. As their beloved daughter, it's a raw and harsh truth to understand as an adult that their relationship was toxic. My mom was independent, resilient, wise and dominant. My dad was giving, affectionate and mild-tempered. They both were attractive with welcoming personalities. Still the two obviously did not provide for one another the stability to feel safe enough in life to grow as individuals and as partners, or to help heal emotional holes for one another. My dad spent some time in the army before living the rest of his life as an alcoholic, and I would say my mom was addicted to under-serving relationships. She started having kids just as she reached her teen years and I was her last child that came as she said goodbye to her thirties. When my dad drank, his personality was quite the opposite of his sober self and it triggered my mom to the point of abuse. My drunk dad was loud and over affectionate, but mostly just obnoxious. He would agitate her and she would react with anger-driven violence. I would say that they fought when he drank, but the truth is she fought him. In most cases, he was too drunk to defend himself, but also, the one thing sober him and intoxicated him had in common, was his lack of aggression.

He wasn't completely innocent however. I recall one incident in particular when he stole her car while heavily under the influence and totaled it. If my memory serves me correctly, the car was pretty new and she was definitely more hurt than angry. That was them though, a sort of topsy-turvy long lived-out love affair. By the time I was 13 years old, the relationship dissolved and they both went on to have new relationships in their lives. However, It was always apparent that they never stopped caring for each other. My mom was diagnosed with colon cancer when I was 15 years old. She fought through it for a couple of years before experiencing remission. Then at the end of my junior year in high school, we lost my dad to heart failure. Shortly after that, her cancer returned and 3 years after losing my dad, I lost my mom too. My mom left this side of eternity just four years shy of experiencing her youngest daughter become a mom...

Different from me, but much like me also, Jaden's recollection of his parents will not be that of a love story. That saddens me for him. Though it would not be fair to edit the beginning of his origin story, my hope has always been anchored in the possibility of love finding me in time for him to know of a different reality and leave him with a different context. I never experienced seeing my mom being emotionally safe enough to be soft as a woman. I never experienced her being functionally loved; no dates, no nice gifts, no opened doors, no conflict resolution or effective communication or evening talks on the couch filled with laughter or no support of dreams. I want something different for my manchild. My parents lived out life as it was handed to them and I believe they existed in spaces as well as they personally knew how. While they both came from two parent households, I can't be sure of what events in their lives manifested in the dysfunctional relationship they shared. I want my son to know that despite the events of my single motherhood and lack of a functional black-love model, I shielded him as best I knew how until I became positioned to proudly experience love with him as my audience of one.

Raising My Manchild

For two years now, my son has witnessed his mom be different, dated and dreamy-eyed. He has had an adolescent's first-hand account of a "boy meets girl, girl likes boy" scenario that has responsibly paced and progressed. He may not have the deeper awareness at his age, but he is witnessing a critical transition take place for both him and his single mom. His origin story is changing...

It is okay and natural to want companionship, even as a single parent. I know society tells us that we shouldn't be focused on relationships, instead we should be "knee deep" in being a perfect parent. Shame on anyone who openly admits the desire to be loved while they parent, right? Wrong! We are human first. It is very healthy to desire companionship. You can be an excellent parent and still have natural desires that you pursue at the same time. If you are a parent that is truly "all in" with how you are raising your child(ren), most days you deplete all of yourself by pouring into your babies. You leave no love unshared. However, the saying goes, "you can't pour from an empty vessel." Who refills your love tank? Right here is where my saved friends would tell me, "God". Yes, we know God is a friend to the friendless. There is no need that He can't meet. However, God has made us humans that are fulfilled by Him through other humans as it concerns our natural desire for companionship and affection. You are not flawed for wanting to be loved in a way that your child(ren) cannot provide. God made you that way. Some may also argue that the great reward of seeing your child(ren) happy should be enough. To them I would simply say, "it's not". Having a companion and parenting partner is a valid desire and a desire that has substantial benefits to not only the single parent, but to the child(ren) as well. So don't muffle how you feel to be accepted by others. Want what you want and make no apologies about it. Just hold on, even in this, God is going to give you the desires of your heart. My only advice is to remember balance and be responsible in your pursuit.

Raising My Manchild

I was recently reading a children's book for my Youtube channel and one sentence struck me as profound. "Children have to live with adult decisions." No truer words ever spoken, right? If we live our lives with this thought at the forefront of our mind, I think we would make a lot less careless decisions as parents. Be mindful of what you are exposing your child(ren) to. As adults, we can recall probably countless traumas we endured that we could have done without and had no action in causing. Call them out to yourself, write them down even. Then ask yourself, "what unnecessary traumas have I inflicted on my child(dren)?Even if trauma may not be the best term for the experiences we have chartered our kids through...I believe if we are more conscious of the fact that we are writing the content of their origin story, we will be more careful with those experiences and the decisions we make that create them.

It is not always the easiest feat to equally feed both the mom side and the woman side of yourself. Both of them have needs that are sometimes hard to juggle. Having a companion does feed both sides. Just make sure that there is no neglect of the mom side to allow the woman side of you to be fulfilled. Be mindful of the residue your decisions leave behind on your child(ren), and let your guiding question be "What do you want their origin story to consist of?"

Finding love as a single mom is never going to be a black and white process. You will likely dirty up that origin story and that's okay, as long as you are not reckless. Forgive yourself and learn from the losses and be intentional about eventually winning at love for the benefit of both you and your child(ren).

Chapter 11:
A Change Is Gonna Come

"The heart of a father is a masterpiece of nature."
~Abbe Provost

There have been so many nights of crying, so many days of wanting to give up, so many desperate thoughts of failure and feeling alone along this journey as a single mom! I am not at all far removed from the head space of feeling like there just wouldn't be a happily ever after for me. Honestly, I pray I never forget actually. I don't ever want to forget what I've been through along this journey. As long as I remember, I will not only remain grateful but I will always be able to uplift a fellow mom. I can remember being in a mental place of beginning to work through accepting defeat. The question I had to consider was "if God doesn't do it, does he love me any less?" It's a real question that really can be applied to any part of life that you are struggling in and it helps to shift your perspective. If God says that my journey through motherhood is to be done completely alone, despite my desire to do it with a partner, is He not still the God that I learned about in church whose concerns are mine? Is He the God of yes and amen if what I'm experiencing in life is Him saying no? Is He saying no or just not yet? If He is saying no, how do I resolve the conflict of that reality against my desire? My final answer was yes. Yes, He was still the same God who had done so much for me. It has been so many needs I've had as a single mom and God has provided every time. He has brought so many people into my life that have blessed me and my child, mostly financially and definitely mentally and emotionally as a bi-product. So after all the years of experiencing him as a provider for us, why would I discount His will for my life because He didn't provide this one thing, a partner?

So I moved forward with a hope to be at peace with where I was in my life as a mom and an individual who wanted to move past being consumed by thoughts of what I didn't have in life. My focus became gratitude. I wanted gratitude to fill up the air all around me. I wanted it thick on my skin. I've known about the law of attraction and the "I AM" factor that many motivational speakers and pastors reference. However, I can't say that the principals truly dwelled in my psyche. Here I was now though, in the middle of a mind shift. I remember practicing meditation and speaking out mantras and affirmations. During this time I had also lost some of the conventional beliefs I have held about religion. While I am not suggesting it's the route to take for anyone else, it's the route God decided was fit for me. This allowed me to open myself up to other unconventional positive reinforcement practices, that I firmly believe helped in my process of shifting my mindset. I researched and introduced myself to crystals and the openness that I can have faith in God and be accepting of the belief that the properties of crystals can direct my energy. For me personally, this new spiritual enlightenment did not disconnect me from God, it really freed me of the boundaries I placed on God as a "church girl". I felt so much lighter in my spirit in this season. So, as confused as I sometimes was dealing with the internal conflict of learning a new way to know God, I sat in it. I'd like to believe that this was the exact destination God needed me to arrive at before someone else could hold space in my life. All the many times I heard people say "you had to first be content in your singleness before God would bless you with a man", I refused to accept it. My desire to have a family and have a significant other was my truth. I didn't understand how God could give me my heart's desire, if I had to first no longer desire it. I thought that was the dumbest advice ever! Now here I am saying that is exactly what happened. As I write these words, it was four years ago that I learned a discipline in focusing more on gratitude than on my wants more than I ever had. It was that discipline that helped me understand what contentment really is. My desire didn't have to leave, my mindset had to change. Not very long into this season, I met a man. I met the man who would change the course of my journey. All these years of fighting to survive and doing my best to kick ass at being a single mother, and today I can no longer own the title single mom. For the first time in my son's life, he has parents and I have a partner.

In my best church "sangin" voice, The storm is over now! Right? I mean this is it. This is the moment I have dreamed of, hoped for, prayed for, advance-shouted for and everything. Help is here! It's smooth sailing from here. Right? *Right?* "Not. So. Fast..." says life.

The metamorphosis of blending into one family has been easy in most regards. It has helped to have like-minds about values and goals and even just the mutual understanding that communication and respect has to be primary for not just our relationship but also our approach to parenting bonus children. With that, we have had to learn new ways of both parenting and communication. By far, parenting has been the biggest challenge of our relationship. Don't get me wrong, we both have amazing kids. They are the same age with a two month difference and couldn't be any more different but get along great. I believe part of the credit of the ease of our blend goes to us not forcing each other on the kids and taking our time to merge them into the fold after we first created safe spaces for one another. I also believe that the main credit goes to God of course for having our union in mind when he created each of us. The kids do have their normal teenage problems, and dealing with them as they arise has exposed differences in our parenting techniques. In discovering these differences,we've also learned that they have to be adjusted for the longevity of our relationship and the success of our children. Still, the orchestration of this "thing of ours" has been somewhat ideal. Yet, while it's natural for me to bask in the newness and effortless cohesion of our new family and breathe a theoretical sigh of relief for having wholeness in the regard of a family, my hallelujahs in my spirit had to take a pause...

What I didn't consider is that my fatherless child of sixteen years would now have to adjust to having an in-house father figure, and that would conjure up unresolved, unacknowledged reservations about the relationship he does not have with his dad. I have spent years being worried about all the ways *not* having a relationship with his dad would affect him and this was just not on my radar. Had it not been for him starting to act out emotionally and seeing an even steeper decline in his academics that were far past what we had ever experienced before, I wouldn't have even thought there was an issue. So in the moment that it becomes a reality that my son has to do extra work outside of the norm to process how another man can come into his life willing and ready to love him as his own, yet his own dad continues to reject him...I'm defensive and angry all over again like the abandonment just happened. It's the domino effect for me! Ugh... it's moments like this that I wish people who feel like single moms of fatherless children should just "get over it already", could experience it for themselves to see how disrespectful that dismissiveness really is. Because when a man decides to not father his manchild, it's layers of negative causes and effects that the child has to live through.

There would be no way around my son having to adjust to the different parenting styles or even just the in-home presence of a man when it has only been me and him his entire existence. He shouldn't have the added emotional pressure of trying to reconcile the conflict that lies between the lack of connection from his biological father and the sincere desire for a connection from a man who has no buy-in into investing in him. Even if it's said that the relationship this man has with me is the buy-in, I say men take interest in women every day and choose not to connect with their child(ren). That's a fact that can very well be proven. Even in some cases where men respect the space their mate has with her children, they don't always choose to love those children as their own. They don't always dig knee-deep into the rearing of the child(ren) in the situation. Relationship with me or not, my son now has a bonus dad who intentionally chooses him every day, outside of our relationship. He invests in creating a safe space and bonds with him separate from our relationship. His correction doesn't look like mine. Yet, it's pure enough for my teenage son to recognize via his own intellect and thought that it comes from a place of love and care. This said even with the admission that my son doesn't like the way his bonus dad corrects him, because it's not what he is used to. Despite that, he can see the good in it. That says something. The challenge to let his bonus dad in still exists because of the internal conflict created by the absence of his biological dad. This is coupled with having to now share his mom, whom he has always had sole proprietorship over. For my son, the order or balance of nature has been disturbed for him as it concerns relationships with men, and possibly relationships period.

My priority as we settle into our blended life has been and will be for some time to reassure him as much as I reasonably can that he is still safe although such a major life change has occurred. I am still the same protective mom who fought to shield him from the inconsistency and outright lies and disregard of his dad. Only now, my protection has been redirected from shielding to carefully exposing him and allowing him to navigate his way through our new reality alongside me. Some days it's easy. Some days it's not only hard but scary. I sometimes fear that the resentment towards me that I've been intentionally working to prevent him from developing (as a result of him not having a relationship with his dad), will reinvent itself as resentment towards me for bringing someone else...a man...into our lives. I know that as parents we can do all that is within our power to raise our kids to be one way and they still choose another way. So, I'm aware that although I have purposefully moved along in our journey as mother and son, choosing him and my peace over being right and being heard, he could still one day decide that from his perspective, I didn't do it right. While I don't see that as a likely outcome for us (because he is older and we have had conversations where I have had the privilege of hearing his heart and witnessing a growth and maturity about our situation), I know that in the unfortunate event of him hypothetically feeling that way, it wouldn't completely break me. It wouldn't break me because I know without doubt that I protected him from years of deeper abandonment insecurities and I've welcomed a sincere, consistent and functioning love into both our lives. He now has not only his mom's protection, but the protection and tutelage of a man who has vowed to hold him up as his own.

This is no fairytale ending. They are not super close or magically in sync and in common to one another. However, they are both comfortable, happy and willing. There is mutual respect between them and their communication continues to develop. They engage in their own talks without me having to be a moderator and they share humorous moments. While one is hip-hop and the other anime, they highly regard and appreciate each other as individuals. The goal has never been to erase and replace the malfunctioned dad, but rather to close the gap on all the many needs that go unmet when a man decides not to father his own child. I am blessed to say that my son is now a boy who has fewer needs not being met and someone of his same gender, someone who stands in the void space where his dad should be, nurturing him in a way that only a man can do.

God's timing is perfect. It's a phrase that you have to experience for yourself to truly be comforted by it. That's the unfortunate truth of the matter. I hated when people told me that! In my opinion, God had surely forgotten that me and my manchild were on this earth roughing it out and in need of a man to balance our family scale. What was the hold up?! To me, God's timing was in a different time zone than mine and nothing about that was perfect. My son was getting older, my patience thinner and my hope lessened. I couldn't understand how it was happening so timely for other single moms in my life, but your girl just couldn't catch a break. knowing that my desire for a man was not a selfish one, why wouldn't God deliver me already? The simple answer is...God's timing is perfect.

While I thought so many times that I was at my breaking point of motherhood, God continued to sustain me and renew my grace for the journey. I wholeheartedly believe that everything my son and I have gone through up to now needed to happen just the way it did, in the amount of time that it did in order for us to be who we are today and who we will be over time. I believe the same for you and your child(ren)! God is truly omniscient. He knows our beginning from our end. He set me and my son up, the same way He is setting you up. I know it doesn't feel like it when we are in the thick of our hell season, but His time is perfect. He is pressing you and molding you to fit your latter days. I'm telling you what I now know for myself.

In conversations, me and my man discovered that our lives were running parallel to one another for some time. At one point we even lived in the same apartment complex. For me, the time that I lived in that particular place, I was barely a year into my motherhood journey and the most depressed and discouraged I probably have been as a mom. If you recall from earlier chapters, I was bitter and angry the first years of being a mom. He on the other hand was already married at that time. If I ever laid eyes on him as a stranger during that time, I couldn't tell you. I was too blinded by bitterness to know. What I can tell you is that I'm thankful that wasn't our time. I am the supreme valuable life partner that I am today because of who I had to be as a single mom. Being a single mom 'made' me. I can also tell you that every day we continue to grow to know each other more and more, I see that the way he loves me and my son is a direct result of how his life experiences have made him. God groomed us, our kids included. He prepared us for the family he knew we would one day be. Our most difficult challenges were not for nothing. We needed to be the people we are today for our union to adhere. It wasn't going to work any other way.

If you have not yet found the man that will love you and your child(ren) as his own in such a healthy way, let me encourage you that God's timing really is perfect. He is going to blow your mind! If you have that man already and maybe you are where I am, navigating through the growing pains of a blended family, remember that God's grace is sufficient. Give yourself grace and teach your family to offer each other grace as you all learn your way. Change is not constant. Blending as a family has taught me a new level of flexibility and compromise. It has caused me to be more aware about my perspectives and opportunities and to be more open minded. Be willing to grow, but remember along the way that growth is rarely comfortable.

Chapter 12:
Giants Do Fall

"Your willingness to wrestle with your demons will cause your angels to sing."
~August Wilson

There is a simple but weighted 'old folks saying' that you may be familiar with. "A watched pot never boils". Scientifically, it takes a pot of water about 8 minutes to reach its boiling point. Eight minutes is not a long time. However, if you stand there watching it, it really does seem like time stands still, especially if you are hungry and cooking a quick meal that requires the water to be at boiling temperature in order to prepare it. This analogy is much like being a single mom and waiting on your co-parenting situation to evolve. I said it before and I will say it again, one of the thoughts I wrestled with the most was "why is it happening for other single moms in my life and not for me"? For over sixteen years now, I have felt as if I was watching a pot of water refuse to boil. Sixteen years doesn't seem like much time when presented in comparison to 40 years of age, much like the 8 minutes it takes for water to boil. However, From the perspective of a single mom of a 17 year old who has been longing for a relationship with his absent dad, Sixteen years is closer to a lifetime. Both myself and my son have been hungry for a more positive co-parenting reality, but again, a watched pot never boils. The saying communicates to us that time is better served focusing on other things, choosing to be productive in another space until the desired outcome we are waiting for happens.

It has been my intentional focus these last few years to fight for a more stable existence for us. In that time I have watched my fatherless son grow into a huge part of the man he will be in his absoluteness. I can remember so vividly possessing such a stubborn fear that I wouldn't know what to do as this manchild's mom before he took his first breath. If I allow myself, I can even revisit the physical and emotional sadness of the time of our journey when he was old enough to express his own sadness caused by his dad's absence. In a moment's notice that past anger can still creep back into my flesh and I find myself visiting his young stuck mom who was lost in her bitterness. The years of me not knowing exactly how to get us free of the grips of poverty are not at all distant for me. In fact, time is truly fleeting when I consider our time together on this path. Time favored us once I took my eyes off the "pot" long enough to charter us out of the wilderness of hopelessly wanting things to be different between him and his dad. I have so much pride in knowing that he has been afforded a front row seat in seeing me fight for our future by refusing to give up on my dreams for both of us. Dreams of education, love, a career and emotional and financial stability. Even before the term existed, I have always desired to reclaim my time, the time that becoming someone's baby mama had stolen from me. Now it would appear that by way of opening up ourselves and redirecting our attention to no longer focusing on daddy deadbeat, it is now my son's turn to reclaim *his* time in the situation.

Under the counsel and guidance of his mentor, my son recently made the decision to reach out to his dad in a final attempt to hold him accountable for the absence in his life. Of course I was not thrilled or optimistic about this decision. That's not to say that I didn't want it to happen or didn't agree with it. I believe that it is not only a very mature position my son has taken, but a necessary one for the management of his own emotional wellbeing. As he has taken the first steps in building this bridge he has my full support and admiration. However, that doesn't remove the very real feelings of anxiousness that I have when I think about all the ways this could go wrong and further damage my son. History has proven his dad highly likely to disappoint him. I won't ever be so positive and forward thinking that I can cheer for the possible devastation of my son. What I can and will continue to do is make my support visible and authentic. While I will occasionally ask for a basic update, I do not pry. I simply let him share what he feels comfortable sharing and I give positive positive feedback and we put a pin in it. It's important that I make him feel comfortable sharing with me as he braves this challenge. What I know is years of him experiencing my anger towards his dad, has made him a protector of my feelings as he has gotten older. He knows that the disregard and neglect or avoidance his dad has historically displayed towards him is a major trigger for me and while I won't get irate and belittle his dad to his face, I will call a spade a spade with no apology. I understand that puts him in a conflicting position, because while he is at an age of awareness about his dad's abandonment, he is still a child who wants to have a relationship with his dad. Especially when he continues to have a relationship with his brother who has a seemingly close bond with their dad. Therefore, I believe he sometimes tows the line between speaking openly and honestly and guarding me. This should not be his role. He should not have to feel the need to mediate between two adults and I own my part in this being the case for us. I think naturally boys develop a sense of committed nurturing towards their mom when there is no man present and possibly even when there is. So I know part of this is just that. Still it's important that he doesn't feel so much a sense of responsibility over my emotions that it causes him to sacrifice his own.

It is early in this new venture my son is on. However, I can't be any more proud of him for taking on this task. He has managed to have the courage and dignity that his dad hasn't been able to possess in his lifetime. I hope that despite the outcome, this will always be something that he can be proud of himself for and something that solidifies for him the grandness of his character as he lives out his years. This very act speaks to the character of the adolescent I have raised! I'd like to believe that genetically he is a combination of all the best parts of myself and his dad. I know that realistically, he will inherit some of our less favorable traits as well. What I am witnessing as he further develops is that he is such a great person. He is mannerable and clever, funny and intriguing and he is considerate and tolerant. He is so comfortable in being uniquely him sometimes even to a fault. Material things have never been impressive to him and he has always been appreciative of what he has. These are just a few examples of the evidence that single motherhood has worked in my favor.

I'm often just proud of us. We have managed to make it seventeen years and counting. We have done a big thing, a thing that I wasn't so sure could be done starting out. We have not only survived, but we have defied the stereotypes that society would attempt to label us with and we have overcome so many obstacles. I pat myself on my back and congratulate myself. With the celebration of making it through single motherhood so far, there is still more living to do and I'm aware of that. I will keep approaching this journey of us knowing that the hardest part is complete. Now I'm nearing the season where I get to see how well my "experiment" worked. I say experiment because of course parenting be it done single or a part of a pair is really intentional trial and error. We don't always get it right. I will give myself grace though knowing that for me, it has always been about doing things right, not being right.

Don't lose time watching and waiting for the donor to all of a sudden get it right. That time may never come. Yet, focus on creating the life you want for you and your child(ren) if no other person ever joins your life. Put your energy into ensuring the present is as best as it could be for where you all are in your journey. Don't let that "pot of water" continue to distract your parenting productivity. This is the formula for creating room for both you and your child(ren) to grow beyond your circumstance. This is the formula that continues to work for me. So, I'm telling you what I know to be tried and true. Let the good that you have in front of you encourage you to keep going. That will sometimes be easier said than done, just know that it's possible and it works.

The time will come when God will pull you right up out of the disappointment you have experienced, waiting on your co-parenting situation to be better. You will one day only give energy to all that is right and working out for you and your child(ren). Let that be your resting place as you continue to thrive as a single mom. God will indeed work the rest out.

If the time comes that your child(ren) wants to reach out to their dad, let me encourage you. It's not an easy place to be. The thoughts of what could go wrong will surely take you back to the place of feeling helpless and like you are leaving your child(ren) standing unguarded. Here's the thing though, allow all the hard work that you have poured into raising a good person to come into play. Give them room to grow into their own character through the circumstance. I know you are just like me, you don't want to ever be the reason they don't have a relationship with their dad. Keep that in mind when you want to intervene. Be their support and let what will be, grow into existence. Even if the outcome is not favorable, they will learn and grow from it. It will either confirm for them that what you have protected them from all these years is something not even worth tangling with, or it will show them that people and situations can and do change.

Chapter 13:
Be Encouraged

"Here's to strong women. May we know them, may we be them, may we raise them."
~Unknown

If my words have gotten you to this page, I salute you! Thank you for being here, not just for me but for yourself. You are so much stronger than you could have ever imagined at the beginning of your journey. You are someone that many are proud of. One of the many things that I've learned in my journey as a single mom is that someone is always watching and whether we know or not, we are encouraging someone. Let this be motivation to keep going. Keep going, yes because someone who needs you is watching, but keep going also because a wiser, stronger, bolder you stands waiting at the end of your journey, excited to greet you. See to it that you exceed her wildest expectations.

It is my absolute honor to have placed myself in your life as your Baby Mama Fairy Godmother! Thank you for being open to me sharing my story with you, that it may encourage you along your own journey. The very reason I started writing this book was because I thought about the often misrepresented us. Those of us who make a conscious decision daily to not be the baby mama of stereotypical storylines. We matter! I thought about those who may not have the biggest support system and sometimes find themselves lonely and discouraged by constantly feeling like you are fighting an endless battle. You are not alone in your effort to fight for what is right for you and your child(dren). Keep fighting, we are rooting for you!

It may often feel like no one gets it. I still remember feeling like my situation was an anomaly but as I grew through it, I understood that God made my situation different to set me up for my purpose. He is setting you up too. You might be the only one that you know of dealing with the turmoil that exists in your situation, but I promise you are not alone. Someone somewhere is or will have a parallel experience and at some point, you will cross paths with them and be a light to their darkness. So be encouraged in knowing that there is a sure purpose in your pain. Don't give up. Do continue to do the necessary selfwork to be a better you. That will renew the strength you need to make you an even better mom. For me, I have started therapy for myself. I want to be my son's first example of what a whole, healthy individual looks like. I want to release some of my lifetime trauma so that I can have room to love him more efficiently. I wish I had the knowledge and courage to seek therapy sooner. I think some of the healing I had to blindly stumble upon could have come easier had I been in therapy as a young mom. Either way, I return to the awareness now that my journey happened the way it did to get me here. Part of my purpose in not getting professional help earlier in my motherhood may be for me to help you get to it earlier in yours. So consider what you need to at this moment to be even better at parenting and don't stop until you receive just that.

If nothing else encourages you, know that you are and will always be the greatest thing that happened to your child(ren). You are the reason they are here and the reason they are growing to be their best self. The work of your hands as a mom is not only priceless, it is divine. Hold hope and pride equally in knowing that what their dad didn't have the strength to do alongside or in partnership with you, you are excelling at by yourself. Even when it doesn't feel like it, you are kicking ass at raising your greatest contributions to mankind. Congratulations!

Wherever you are and whatever season you are in as a single mom, I send you strength and I send you support. I boldly raise my glass in your honor, because I know you are doing your best to be your best for your child(dren). Fight on...

Meet the Author

Author T. Grow is a native of Prichard, AL. She moved to Huntsville, AL to attend her beloved HBCU, Alabama Agricultural & Mechanical (A&M) University in 1999, where she became a single mom in 2004. After later receiving her Bachelor's Degree in Business Administration from Faulkner University in 2012, she completed her Master's Degree in Early Childhood Education, back at Alabama A&M University in 2017. Since, she has been committed to living out her dreams as a thriving mom, an author and classroom teacher as well as working as the executive assistant at Real Fathers Making A Difference, Inc.

Raising My Manchild is T. Grow's fourth published title. It follows *True Witness; A Compilation of Gospel Plays, Luci the Love Bug and Alice Leaves the Palace*, her two children's books.

For more information, connect with T. Grow.

Social Media | @AuthorTdotGrow

Website | www.tdotgrow.com

T. Grow would love to speak to the women at your next event!

For booking inquiries, contact LaToya@tdotgrow.com

They don't want you to win.

Do it anyway.

Made in the USA
Columbia, SC
16 June 2021